Tipsy Treats

Tipsy Treats

Alcohol-Infused Cupcakes, Marshmallows, Martini Gels, and More!

Autumn Skoczen

Skyhorse Publishing

Skyhorse Publishing books may be purchased in bulk at special discounts for sales promotion, corporate gifts, fund-raising, or educational purposes. Special editions can also be created to specifications. For details, contact the Special Sales Department, Skyhorse Publishing, 307 West 36th Street, 11th Floor, New York, NY 10018 or info@skyhorsepublishing.com.
Skyhorse® and Skyhorse Publishing® are registered trademarks of Skyhorse Publishing, Inc.®, a Delaware corporation.

www.skyhorsepublishing.com

10 9 8 7 6 5 4 3 2 1

Library of Congress Cataloging-in-Publication Data is available on file.

Cover design by Sarah Brody
Cover photo © Larry Skoczen

Print ISBN: 978-1-63220-692-3
Ebook ISBN: 978-1-63220-993-1

Printed in China

Contents

Introduction

The idea of putting alcohol into baked goods is nothing new. In fact, cultures have been merging the two together for decades; one example is rum cake. What *is* new is the manipulation of alcohol into sugary goods that crosses the lines between safe and sober.

Traditionally, alcohol is used in the cooking or baking process prior to adding heat. That means when the temperature rises, the actual alcohol content evaporates and you are left with the gentle fragrance and taste of what was once intoxicating. This way, those under the legal age limit for alcohol consumption can enjoy the dessert, but adults might still want the effects of alcohol in their sweets, and that's where our story begins . . .

Who wants to eat a cupcake where the alcohol was baked out, or whose flambé seared off their eyebrows along with their liquor? There is no point in being an adult if you can't indulge in all the things we worked so hard to enjoy . . . After all, we did have to wait an agonizing twenty-one years before being legally allowed to even taste the stuff!

In this book, we take the liquor out of the martini glass and put it into all its different forms so that we can enjoy every last drop. I will teach you simple tricks, give you creative ideas, and offer lots of guidance so that you can easily recreate these recipes in your own home.

But first, we have to start with the basics . . .

The Basics of Baking with Alcohol

You can't cook with your favorite bottle of liquor without first knowing the facts. A great rule of thumb is that if you run into a snag, come back to this portion and re-read it. You will most likely figure out your mistake.

Rule #1: Never add heat to your alcoholic confection!
Alcohol starts to boil at 172°F, but it will start to evaporate the minute it hits a heat source that is less than 20°F below the boiling point. In fact, alcohol begins to evaporate the minute it meets air, just like water except a little bit faster. There are a few variables that will affect the rate of evaporation including, airflow, temperature (humidity levels), and exposed surface area.

An open bottle of liquor on your counter won't evaporate as quickly as it would if it was poured onto a baking sheet. Likewise, dry air will also speed up the process as opposed to more humid conditions. And if you put a flame to it, you'll say good-bye to that alcohol quicker than you can say "I need another cocktail!"

Depending on who you talk to, some may argue that cooking alcohol still doesn't burn off all the alcohol content completely. While this may be true to some sort of scientific extent, there will *still* be more alcohol in your vanilla extract than there will be left in your dessert. Besides, when it comes down to it, it doesn't take a scientist to be able to detect that there really is or isn't alcohol left in your dessert . . . So let's just leave that argument for the tastebuds to decide.

I noticed throughout my baking career that I very rarely had a thermometer on hand, let alone the time to be trying to figure out at what point the alcohol was too hot, or when it was boiling . . . the hell with all that!

So that is how I developed rule number one.

Rule #2: Stick with what you like. You will be much happier with the outcome.

We will also get into all the different varieties and forms of alcohol.

We have:

- Liquor
- Liqueurs
- Wine
- Beer

Actually, if you talked to a pro, they would tell you there are only three classifications: beer, wine, and spirit, but the only thing we are professional at is the consumption so we can veer a bit on this one, right?

I like to break it down into categories because sugar and water are the biggest differences in these categories and those two ingredients just so happen to be big players in the world of baking.

Let's go over the literal definitions:

Liquor: Hard liquor, or spirit, is an alcoholic beverage that is produced by distillation of a mixture produced by alcoholic fermentation. (The higher the alcohol content, the "harder" the spirit.)

Liqueurs: An alcoholic beverage made from a distilled spirit that is flavored with fruits, herbs, spices, creams, flowers, or nuts, and bottled with added sugar or another sweetener.(Not to be confused with the growing popularity of flavored spirits, like marshmallow vodka. It's a common misconception that the greatest difference is in the alcohol content, but you can find liqueurs upwards of 55 proof. The rule of thumb in distinguishing between the two is that liqueurs are syrupy in consistency and often too sweet or concentrated to drink straight up, not that that has stopped anybody from trying, but liqueurs are typically meant to be mixed with other alcoholic liquids.)

Wine: An alcoholic beverage made from the natural fermentation of grapes or other fruits.

(I know, I just said that liquor is an alcoholic beverage created by fermentation, but liquors are distilled, and wines and beers are not, and unlike liqueurs, which can still produce a pretty high alcohol content, wine and beer are typically less than 10 percent alcohol by volume.)

Beer: An alcoholic beverage produced by saccharification of starch and fermentation of sugar.

(Don't be embarrassed . . . my spell check didn't even know what saccharification was until I added it to my dictionary. It's when a carbohydrate is broken down into its component sugar molecule by hydrolysis. You know, like sucrose being broken down into glucose and fructose.)

I don't feel it's necessary to go into great detail about the fruits, vegetables, and grains that are used to make alcohol, but it's certainly something you will want to research, especially if you are working with a gluten-free diet, and for sugar-free desserts as well.

Here is a brief rundown of the most popular ingredients used to make some of your favorite beverages:

- Barley
- Rye
- Corn
- Wheat
- Rice
- Grapes
- Apples
- Pears
- Plums
- Bananas
- Ginger
- Potatoes
- Sugar Cane
- Honey
- Milk
- Sugar

It will save you lots of time and money to choose one or two of your favorite alcohols and stick with them during each round of baking. There are just some things that don't go well together, and if you don't care for beer out of a can, you most likely won't like it in a cupcake.

Rule #3: Alcohol burns sugar (though you will still taste the sugar). So find a happy medium if you plan on exploring new confections.
You will need to understand how sugar and alcohol react together. Alcohol burns—it literally, makes your mouth feel like it's on fire. So I am sure you can imagine that it does quite a number on sugar.

Too much alcohol and it will "eat" its way through your confection. But of course, not enough and you may as well have not added any at all.

A pretty easy way to tell if you have added too much alcohol is if your solid confection (frosting, pudding, etc.) becomes soupy and unstable. At this point, there is no turning back. The alcohol already has started a reaction with the sugar, and your best bet is just to start from scratch. Don't worry if this happens to you . . . just grab your cocktail, take a sip, and try again!

Tools

These are the basics to getting started with these recipes, and a reference guide in case you come across something that is listed in a recipe that you are unfamiliar with.

Though some of these tools are pretty basic and obvious, there are others that I am suggesting are not necessary to buy, especially if you don't plan on baking too often. If you want the best possible outcome, and most professional-looking bakery, investing in the right tools is essential, and maybe watch a few video tutorials online that will help you learn the crafts of frosting cupcakes.

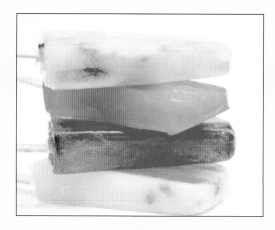

1. Patience. Okay, this may be silly, but one of my biggest mistakes when I started baking at a young age was thinking that I could skip a few steps, or do things "my own way" because I was too impatient to read the directions thoroughly and carefully. Baking is chemistry, and one little slipup can ruin all the time and money you have already put into your recipe. Just take your time, make sure you don't cut corners, and only swap out ingredients if the recipe says so.

2. Cupcake pan. Mini or regular, it's your preference. It's worth making sure you have at least two pans since these recipes will yield more than just twelve standard size cupcakes.

3. Cupcake papers. 1 ⅝ inch is standard for mini-size cupcake papers, my preferred size. You can buy these at your local grocery store or cake supply store. If the paper is too tall, you won't have a nice muffintop to decorate.

If it's too shallow, your cupcake batter will overflow and stick to the pan. Minipans have a tendency to vary in size by a few centimeters, so if you are not sure, measure the base of the cupcake holder and try to match up that size when shopping for papers. Your pan may even say what size they are. It is worth taking the time to get the right papers, since they are literally the glue that holds your cupcakes together! Standard size cupcake paper bases should measure 2 inches.

4. Piping bag. This tool is essential if you expect to have perfectly iced cupcakes. Sure you can use a sandwich bag or coat it on with a butter knife, but some of these recipes won't even allow you to do that because of their whipped and fragile texture. You don't need anything too large, 10 to 14 inches will get the job done. If you plan on baking frequently, I would go with a larger bag so that you are not refilling it constantly.

5. Coupler. This tool is used to pin smaller piping tips onto the bag. It is also nice if you want to interchange piping tips with one bag. I personally think it is easier to pipe with larger tips where you don't need a coupler. You tend to get nicer lines and peaks with larger tips, and it's really only necessary to use smaller, detailed tips if you plan on getting intricate and fancy with your piping.

6. Piping tips. There are two tips that I use almost all the time. A large round tip (Wilton 1a or 2a) will give you round peaks or nice dollops. A star tip (Wilton 1b) will give you pretty petals and edges, a more fancy look, and you can even make simple roses with it. These tips do not need couplers.

7. Mixer. It doesn't matter if it is a hand mixer or a table mixer, but for the best possible outcome, plan on having an electric device that will do the mixing for you. It is most ideal if you have the ability to use a paddle and whisk attachment, which is why table mixers are the best. Each recipe will say when it calls for a different attachment, and why.

8. Spatula. A firm, flat-edged spatula will make your work much easier. All you need is one.

9. Measuring cups. Make sure you use liquid cups for liquid and standard cups for solids.
10. Measuring spoons.
11. Ice cream scoop. There are two sizes depending on the size cupcakes you are baking. For mini cupcakes, use ¾-ounce scoop or even a bit smaller. For standard size use 1 ⅝-ounce scoop. For minis, your scoop will only need to be filled about half way. For standard size, you will want your scoop to be level.

Tips & Tricks

BAKING TIME

Every oven cooks differently. My electric oven may cook these recipes perfectly at 2 minutes, but yours may need a few extra minutes . . . or maybe a few minutes less. Environment and weather also play a factor. It may take a bit longer to bake in high humidity areas as opposed to drier climates. Instead of taking each step of these recipes as a strict rule, experiment a little, and don't be afraid to check on your cupcakes often to determine the perfect cooking time and temperature based on your home and equipment. If your cupcakes are burning at the bottom, but still undercook on top, then turn the heat down to about 325°F. If they are burning on the top but are raw on the inside, then lower your oven rack. Last but not least, don't get frustrated if the first or second batch doesn't turn out too well. If you're a beginning baker, start with a basic vanilla recipe so that you are not using up expensive ingredients. That way, if you have to play around with a few batches to figure out your settings perfectly, it won't be a big deal if you end up having to throw them away.

BEATING VERSUS WHISKING

When a recipe calls for your ingredients to be beaten, you will use the paddle attachment on your mixer. When the recipe calls for your ingredients to be whipped or whisked, you will use the whisk attachment. If you don't have multiple attachments, don't fret. You can always whisk by hand with a handheld whisk. Just pay attention, because the whisk incorporates air into the batter, which will be an essential "ingredient" that will help create a light and fluffy batter.

BLOOMING
This is the process of adding liquid to gelatin, which enlarges the gelatin granules and softens them. This will make sure you end up with a smooth finished product, and eliminates the risk of having a gummy layer in your gelatin.

BUTTER
Bringing to room temperature
The best way to do this is to let your butter sit on a counter top for a few hours until it is soft to the touch. Make sure you are not letting your butter sit near hot surfaces, such as your preheating oven, on top of a microwave, or near other hot appliances. If you forget to leave your butter out to bring to room temperature, place the stick with a paper towel on top on a plate. Microwave for 5 seconds at a time. You want the butter to be soft to the touch, and not melted! Check it after each 5-second interval. Rotate butter if only the bottom is softening more quickly than the top, or vice versa. If you try to use melted butter in your recipe, then you are no longer adding a solid, and are changing the consistency of the batter. The heat will also react with your other ingredients, and you will ultimately have problems with your final product.

Salted versus Unsalted
Almost 100 percent of the time, when baking, a recipe will call for unsalted butter. Why? Because you cannot determine or measure the amount of salt that is inside each stick. Is it the end of the world if you have only salted butter? No . . . but then I would ease up on any additional salt that is called for, and be sure to taste-test your batter to check that you aren't adding too much or too little.

BUTTERCREAM
Crusting versus Standard
This comes down to preference. When I bite into my cupcakes, I love the feeling of soft, smooth frosting with a velvety texture. Others prefer a crusting buttercream, with a thin crusted shell, that breaks when bitten into. Crusting buttercream is also best to use for more stable recipes, for example, dipping your cupcake into ganache, or frosting a cake that will be covered in fondant. However, what it all comes down to is what your palate likes best.

DOUBLE-BOILING
This is the process of heating up a bowl by steam or indirect heat with another bowl that is filled with water. There are lots of ingredients that burn super quickly, like milk and chocolate, and the best way to heat them is by using the double-boiler system. Likewise, there are some recipes that call for this system so that the ingredients don't overcook (like eggs) or to prevent caramelization (like sugar). I used to think that I had to go out and buy a special double boiling pot (which they do make, and you are welcome to buy if you so please), however, you can create your own double boiler by using the pots and bowls you have at home. My preferred method is using a larger saucepan. I will fill this pan about a quarter of the way with water. However, the rule of thumb when trying to decide how much water to add is the water should just barely be touching, or not touching at all, the bottom of the second bowl/pan. You then take another pan or metal bowl (mixing bowls work great!) that is a little bit smaller than the water pan. It should just rest on the edges of the water pan. You do not want the bottom of the secondary bowl or pan to be touching the bottom of the water pan. You then place your ingredients in the dry bowl, stirring often to help distribute the heat. If you start to notice lots of smoke, then your water may have been completely cooked out of the pan. If water starts to boil over, then you have added too much water, and in both cases the heat is probably too high. The idea is to slowly cook your ingredients at a minimal, but well-dispersed heat, so don't think that just because you are using this system you can increase the heat

to make the process faster. I promise it is worth taking your time, since the results of using a double boiler are often impressive! For obvious reasons, only use metal pans and bowls. Even though the heat on the second bowl is indirect, you will not want to use ceramic, glass, or plastic since the heat could still cause breakage and melting. Only use items that you would place directly over a flame. Be cautious of touching the secondary bowl if there is no handle. It will be hot, and will burn your hands. Use heat-resistant gloves to handle the bowl. Never leave a metal utensil in the double boiler, as it will also conduct the heat rather quickly and will burn you when you try to pick it up.

EGGS

Bringing to Room Temperature

Grab a bowl and fill it with some warm water. Too warm and you will start cooking your eggs. Let the eggs sit in the warm water for a few minutes, until they come to room temperature.

Does it make a difference if they are cold or at room temperature? For most recipes, no, which is good news, but oftentimes if the recipe calls for it, it is necessary. For light cakes, such as chiffon and angel food cake, the cold eggs will prevent the batter from becoming light and fluffy, resulting in a dense cake. So it is well worth taking the extra steps to bring your eggs to room temperature if the recipe says so.

Separating the yolks from the whites

This is a skill that may take a while to master. If you are just learning, make sure to crack your eggs in a separate bowl so that you can pick out egg shells or throw out the egg if you end up breaking the yolk. The best way is to crack the egg down the middle, using each half of the egg shell as its own mini bowl. Gently tip over the shell to let the whites pour out into the bowl, using the empty half of the egg shell to catch the yolk and any remaining whites. Keep flip-flopping the yolk between egg shells until most of the whites have fallen into a bowl and have been removed. You can also use an egg yolk separator, even though I feel these tend to be just as tricky to use. If you accidentally get some yolk into your whites, use a spoon to remove it. If your yolk breaks and you mix the two, just save the broken egg for a different recipe. Your recipe will not turn out well if the recipe calls for just whites and you mix in yolk as well.

FILL-HOLE
Using a round piping tip, insert the smallest part of the tip into the center of the cupcake. Twist the tip as you insert it into the cupcake to help smoothly cut the cake. Pull the tip out, removing the cake center of the cupcake. Discard the removed cake by inserting finger into the opposite end of the piping tip.

FLOUR
Rising versus All-Purpose versus Cake Flour
There are so many choices! Although it may seem like you can easily replace one for the other, understand that they do have some differences that will affect your final product. All-purpose flour is just that, all-purpose! It's universally used in baking because it's common flour without any other ingredients. Self-rising flour comes with salt and baking powder already inside the bag. Recipes that call for self-rising may not call for other leavening agents. Cake flour is a much finer grind, has higher starch content, and lower protein content. Low protein means less gluten, which will result in a much lighter, fluffier cake. This is why it is best to make the extra trip to the store for the right flour since each will react differently to the variable of ingredients being used in the recipe.

FOLDING
A technique used to gently mix ingredients. Folding is done by taking your spatula to the bottom of your batter bowl and lifting the batter up and turning your hand so that it falls back onto the top. Continue to do this until you *just* incorporate the ingredient. Folding is meant to be gentle and minimal. Too much and you will remove the air and deflate your batter. Folding is always done by hand, and never with an electric mixer.

FROSTING
Achieving the Perfect Consistency

The wonderful part about frosting is that it can almost always be fixed should a mistake be made. Did you accidentally add too much milk or butter? Simply add more powdered sugar a small bit at a time until you reach a nice, smooth consistency. Maybe you got a little excited and overdid it on the powdered sugar? All you have to do is add some more milk or water, a tbsp at a time. (You can add milk or water even if the recipe doesn't call for it.)

The perfect consistency should be smooth, silky, lump-free, and if you stick a spoon or finger into the batter and pull it out, a nice peak should form and hold its place. Another way to test consistency is by placing a butter knife into the center of the bowl of frosting. Don't let the knife tip hit the bottom of the bowl.

If the knife stays in place and doesn't budge at all, you have created stiff frosting. This is beneficial in some decorating cases, but ultimately, stiff frosting is harder to pipe out of bags, especially through small piping tips or specialty tips. Stiff frosting will also be pretty resilient to toppings—sprinkles will just bounce off. The only time a stiff frosting is necessary for cupcakes is if you plan on turning the frosted cupcake upside down to dunk into a coating of chocolate syrup, etc. If it's too late and you have to use your batch of stiff frosting, you can lightly mist your cupcakes with water to create a sticky layer that your toppings can adhere too.

If the knife falls or leans over a bit, you have created perfect frosting, with medium consistency. Ideal for frosting your cupcakes, this frosting should be strong enough to maintain its shape once piped, and have a nice finishing peak. It should be sticky enough to catch and hold your toppings as well. If making milk-based or crusting buttercream, it is important that you put your toppings on right away in order to catch the brief period of time where the frosting is still tacky. It tends to crust over pretty quickly, and once crusted, your toppings will not stick.

If the knife falls completely to the side of the bowl, you have created soft frosting, with a loose consistency. This kind of frosting is no good for frosting cupcakes, especially if you plan on transporting them, or if they will be sitting out on a display, especially in warmer climates. Soft frosting has no stability and will appear to be melting before your eyes when piped onto the cupcake. Even if you are somewhere between perfect and soft consistency, I recommend not taking the risk. The last thing you want is for your cupcakes to start melting because of a warm car ride, or sitting out at a picnic.

Keep in mind the conditions your cupcakes will be in prior to being eaten. If you know they will be exposed to outdoor weather, a warm home, or the sun, making frosting that is somewhere between stiff and perfect is just fine! By keeping your finished cupcakes in the fridge for an hour or two prior to transportation, your cupcakes won't be ruined if they fall over, and it will give you some time to get them back into a cool area.

Piping Rules and Common Problems

If you don't mix your frosting well. If you have lumpy powdered sugar or you don't beat the butter or cream cheese completely, it will be impossible to pipe your frosting through any kind of star tip or specialty tip. The lumps will get stuck in those tiny spaces and clog your tips. This also goes for frosting that calls for lumpy additives like nuts and chips that are mixed in. You will want to use a round tip only for these types of recipes. If you really like the star tip look, then remember to *always* beat your butter and shortening first so that they are completely smooth. (This also means making sure your butter is at room temperature.) Sift in your dry ingredients to remove any lumps (dry ingredient lumps are especially common if the sugar has been sitting in your cabinet or container for some time. In this case, sifting is essential for a nice finished product.) And make sure you omit adding any solid ingredients to your frosting. Instead, use those ingredients as toppings.

How to Frost a Cupcake

This topic could become its very own book. The options are endless and everyone has their own preference when it comes to the finished look. You will get the most professional look if you use a piping bag and piping tip. You can practice dollops, swirls, and peaks by piping your frosting onto a dry cookie sheet. When you are done, simply scrap the icing off, place back in a bag or bowl, and reuse . . . over and over. Practice this until you feel confident and ready to pipe directly onto a cupcake. Here are a few key tips for proper frosting techniques:

1. Fill your bag no more than three-quarters of the way full. Too much frosting, and it will become difficult to hold the bag comfortably, and the frosting will likely begin to spill out from the top of the bag. If you find that you are constantly refilling your bag, then purchase one that is a few inches larger.
2. By gently squeezing your bag from the bottom to the top, you will encourage any air bubbles to escape. I like to do this one or two times every time I refill the bag. The bubbles will need to escape somehow, and if you leave them in the bag while you pipe, they will ultimate turn into mini explosions of frosting . . . leaving unsightly holes in your piped frosting.
3. Twist the bag closed, and hold the twisted section tightly with your hand. As you frost, keep twisting the bag closed, removing extra air in the bag and readjusting your hands so that the bag still fits nicely in your palms.
4. When you are ready to start piping, put pressure on the top of the bag (where you are holding the twisted top) instead of squeezing the bottom with your second hand. Not only are you encouraging air bubbles, but you are working backwards by pushing the majority of the frosting back to the top of the bag. If you can't help but want to squeeze at the bottom, then try switching your hands around. Put your squeezing hand at the top and your guiding hand at the bottom.
5. Hold your bag vertical to the cupcake. This will ensure that your frosting is centered. If you notice that your frosting is leaning or lop-sided, be more conscience of your vertical hold and try to look down on the cupcake versus frosting it an angle.

6. Keep the piping tip at least half an inch or so away from the top of your cupcake. Squeeze the bag gently and let the frosting "fall" onto your cupcake. You will guide it by slowly moving your hand in a circular motion, bringing those circles closer together to create a tall peak.When your peak is complete, stop applying pressure to the bag. You can either *gently* press down and lift to complete the peak, or you can quickly swoop the tip away, still moving in a circular direction, to complete your tip. This is the same exact technique for creating dollops, except instead of a circular motion, hold your bag half an inch over the cupcake, apply pressure, and let the frosting fall onto the cupcake. As you fill the cupcake, lift your bag higher to keep the dollop from having a squished appearance. Finish your peak the same as describe above.
7. If you're still having problems or are more of a visual learner, get on the Internet and research video tutorials on how to frost a cupcake.

GANACHE

Ganache is a glaze, icing, sauce, or filling made from chocolate and cream. Ganache is typically made by heating cream and incorporating chunks of chocolate until the chocolate melts and creates a smooth chocolate mixture. You can easily create a thicker (richer) ganache by adding more chocolate or less cream. When the mixture is first made, it will be loose and sauce-like. As it sits, it will become thicker, and will be best used as a glaze. When completely chilled and set, ganache will become super thick. At this point it can be used as a frosting, which will be a nice dark and rich fudge-like consistency. Or you can beat the ganache and turn it into a light and fluffy whipped chocolate frosting. Once ganache has chilled and set, reheating it to turn it back into a sauce or glaze becomes tricky. The chemical reactions have already occurred, and when adding heat, the oils will start to separate, leaving your ganache clumpy and oily. With this in mind, make sure you work fast if you need your ganache to be saucy or a glaze. The best rule of thumb is to just create a new batch if your ganache starts to set before you are done using it to have the best results. Likewise, if your ganache is too syrupy, don't be afraid to let it sit for a few minutes as it starts to thicken. Just make sure to check it often.

NON-REACTIVE DISH

Reactive pans are those that react chemically with food. The most common are aluminum and copper. They conduct heat well and tend to make your food have a funny taste. Non-reactive pans would be made of clay, enamel, plastic, glass, and stainless steel. The last thing you want is for your gelatin to taste like metal or not firm up correctly because of the pan.

PROPANE TORCH

This is a handheld gas device that can easily be used to cook surfaces, such as meringues and brulees. Although you can find these at restaurant supply stores, I find you can save yourself some money by purchasing them at your local hardware store. Size does not matter, however, smaller sizes will make it easier to handle and won't be too heavy to hold for longer periods of time. Is this a necessary tool? Only if you feel you will get a good use out of it, and are aiming to achieve the most professional outcome with your final cupcake appearance.

SIFTING

Sifting helps remove clumps from your dry ingredients, and also adds air. You would be surprised how stubborn flour and sugar clumps can be, and may never dissolve into your batter, so it's worth taking the time to sift your dry ingredients. You can buy a sifter or you can use a fine netted strainer or cheese cloth bag. It may take some time to sift but is worth it when you have a perfectly fluffy cake to eat!

TESTING FOR READINESS

Insert a butter knife or toothpick into cupcake. If the object inserted comes out clean, this mean that the cupcakes are ready. You can also test this by gently touching the top of your cupcakes. If they spring back after a light impression, they are done. If they sink, or batter comes off on your finger, they need more time. No single oven bakes the same, so don't rely on color, especially if you are working with darker batters. Typically, the bottom of a cupcake will burn or overcook long before the top portion becomes brown or has the appearance of being "done."

ZESTING

All you need is a zester, and some patience. When you zest, you want to use just the outer skin of the fruit. Once you start to get to the white part, or the rind, the flavor will become extremely bitter. Zest the entire fruit over a bowl or plate. Because the zest is moist, it is hard to use as a garnish after it has hit a plate. If you want to garnish a cupcake with zest, it is best to zest the lemon directly over your cupcakes. Unfortunately, after you have zested your fruit, you will need to find use for the leftovers, otherwise, it will dry out fairly quickly. You can juice your fruit, eat it, or try to find another item to bake where you can use the rest of the fruit without wasting it.

Alcoholic Cupcakes

Rum Raisin Cupcakes

Ingredients

2.6 oz raisins (your preference in type of raisins)

3 tbsp rum

2 cups self-rising flour

1 tsp baking powder

1 cup unsalted butter (at room temperature)

1 cup granulated sugar

4 eggs (at room temperature)

5 tbsp dark rum

2 tbsp light brown sugar

Instructions

1. Soak raisins in the rum for 3 hours so that they become saturated. They will become fatter in appearance. It's one of those times where you can't cut corners because rum and raisins are a pretty important part of this recipe!
2. Preheat oven to 350°F.
3. Line your cupcake pan.
4. Sift in flour and baking powder in a medium bowl.
5. Add butter and sugar.
6. Use an electric mixer with whisk attachment until the batter is light and fluffy.
7. Add in eggs one at a time; make sure each egg is well incorporated before adding the next.
8. Continue to beat the mixture until smooth and pale on medium-low speed, approximately 2 to 3 minutes.
9. Fold in raisins until just incorporated. Too much folding, and you will deflate the batter you just worked so hard to make fluffy!
10. Fill your cupcake papers about half full.
11. Bake for 22 minutes for full-size, or 12 minutes for mini cupcakes.

12. Use a butter knife or toothpick for testing.
13. Take the cupcake pan out from oven, remove cupcakes, and let chill.
14. To make rum syrup, combine dark rum and brown sugar in a small sauce pan.
15. Simmer the rum syrup for approximately 5 minutes on low heat. (High heat will burn the sugar and ruin the syrup.)
16. Create a fill-hole using a piping tip.
17. Pour the warm rum syrup into the cupcakes, making sure not to over-saturate.
18. Cool cupcakes for another 5 minutes before frosting.

*Recommended frosting: Vanilla buttercream garnished with raisins, or a sprinkle of brown sugar.

Coffee Kahlua Cupcakes

Ingredients

1 cup self-rising flour
1 cup unsalted butter (at room temperature)
1 cup granulated sugar
2 tbsp instant coffee grounds (Regular coffee won't work since it won't dissolve. If you like it strong, add a little more!)
4 eggs (at room temperature)
1 cup chocolate chips

Instructions

1. Preheat oven to 350°F.
2. Line your cupcake pan.
3. Sift flour into a separate mixing bowl and set aside.
4. Use an electric mixer to beat butter until smooth. Add sugar and coffee and whisk the batter until light and fluffy.
5. Add eggs one at a time. Make sure the eggs are beaten well before adding the next.
6. Continue to beat the mixture until smooth and pale on medium low speed approximately 2–3 minutes.
7. Fold in chocolate chips. Stir the batter and chocolate chips until well combined.
8. Fill the papers half-full with a large spoon or scoop.
9. Bake for 22 minutes for full-size, or 12 minutes for mini cupcakes.
10. Use a butter knife or toothpick for testing.
11. Take the cupcake pan out of the oven, remove the cupcakes, and let chill.

(The alcohol for these cupcakes is in the frosting!)
*Recommended frosting: Kahlua frosting. Garnish with a sprinkling of instant coffee, or some chocolate-covered coffee beans.

Strawberry Daiquiri Cupcakes

Ingredients

1 cup dried strawberries, finely chopped (The sugar in fresh strawberries will caramelize during cooking, making your cupcake sticky and practically cake-less. It's best to find dried, or freeze-dried berries instead.)

3 tbsp rum

1 cup unsalted butter (at room temperature)

1 cup granulated sugar

1 cup self-rising flour

1 tsp baking powder

4 eggs (at room temperature)

Syrup:

5 tbsp rum

2 tbsp sugar

Instructions

1. Soak dried strawberries in the rum for at least an hour until they are half soft. If using freeze-dried berries, omit this step. Do *not* discard left over liquid . . . we will use it!
2. Preheat oven to 350°F.
3. Line your cupcake pan.
4. Beat butter until soft and smooth. Add sugar and liqueur leftover from Step 1.
5. Sift in flour and the baking powder.
6. Use an electric mixer to whisk the batter until light and fluffy.
7. Add in eggs, one at a time, making sure each is well incorporated before adding the next.
8. Continue to beat the mixture until smooth and pale on medium low speed approximately 2–3 minutes.
9. Fold in soaked strawberries. Stir the batter and strawberries until well combined.

10. Fill your papers half full with large spoon or scoop.
11. Bake for 22 minutes for full-size, or 12 minutes for mini cupcakes.
12. Use a butter knife or toothpick for testing.
13. Take the cupcake pan out of oven and make 3–6 holes in each cupcake.
14. To make syrup, combine rum and sugar in a pan.
15. Simmer the syrup for approximately 5 minutes on low heat. (Low heat! Too high and you will burn off the alcohol!)
16. Pour or coat the warm syrup over the cupcake.
17. Let the cupcakes cool completely before frosting.

*Recommended frosting: Strawberry buttercream. Garnish with some fresh strawberries.

Apple Pie Cupcakes

Ingredients

½ cup butter (at room temperature)
½ cup granulated sugar
2 large eggs, at room temperature
½ cup self-rising flour
½ cup unsweetened apple sauce
1 tbsp ground cinnamon
½ cup chopped pecans

1 cup raisins
1 apple (sliced)
2 tbsp granulated sugar

Apple Brandy Drizzle:
4 tbsp Apple Brandy
3 tbsp granulated sugar

Instructions

1. Preheat oven to 350°F.
2. Line your cupcake pan.
3. Beat the butter until smooth.
4. Use an electric mixer and add sugar. Mix with butter until fluffy and pale.
5. Add one egg at a time, making sure each egg is well incorporated before adding the next.
6. Sift in the flour. Beat the mixture until smooth and pale on medium-low speed for approximately 2–3 minutes.
7. Fold apple sauce, cinnamon, pecans, and raisins into batter until just incorporated.
8. Fill the papers half-full with large spoon or scoop.
9. Decorate each cupcake with apple slices. (Toss the apple slices in some lemon juice to prevent them from turning brown.)
10. Bake for 25 minutes for full-size, or 12–14 minutes for mini cupcakes.
11. Use a butter knife or toothpick for testing.

To make the Apple Brandy Drizzle: Combine apple brandy and granulated sugar in a saucepan. Simmer gently until sugar is completely dissolved (it should be a medium thickness consistency). If too loose, add more sugar. If too stiff, add a small amount of brandy until you reach the desired consistency.

Drizzle the icing onto the cooled cupcakes as is, or frost the cupcakes first and drizzle the syrup onto the top of the frosting. Make sure your syrup is relatively cool before pouring onto frosting to prevent the frosting from melting.

*Recommended frosting: Cream cheese frosting. Garnish with some cinnamon.

Chili Chocolate Cupcakes

Ingredients

1 cup unsalted butter (at room temperature)
1 cup self-rising flour
1 tsp baking powder
1 cup granulated sugar
4 eggs (at room temperature)

1 tbsp chilies (unseeded and finely chopped)
1 cup chocolate chips (use mini chocolate chips for mini cupcakes)

Syrup:
5 tbsp vodka
2 tbsp light brown sugar
Chili powder or cayenne powder for garnish

Instructions

1. Preheat oven to 350°F.
2. Line your cupcake pan.
3. Use an electric mixer to beat the butter until light and fluffy.
4. Sift in flour and baking powder. Add sugar.
5. Add eggs one at a time making sure each is well incorporated before adding the next.
6. Continue to beat the mixture until smooth and pale on medium low speed approximately 2–3 minutes.
7. Fold in chilies and chocolate chips until just combined.
8. Fill the papers half full with large spoon or scoop.
9. Bake for 22 minutes for full-size, or 12 for mini cupcakes.
10. Use a butter knife or toothpick for testing.
11. Take the cupcake pan out of oven and make 3–6 holes in each cupcake.

To make the syrup: Combine vodka and brown sugar in a pan. Simmer the vodka syrup for approximately 5 minutes. Make sure to use low heat to keep from burning off the alcohol. Pour or coat the warm syrup over the cupcake, and cool completely before frosting.

*Recommended frosting: Stiff chocolate ganache or chocolate buttercream. Garnish with chili powder dusting.

Mimosa Cupcakes

Ingredients

⅔ cup unsalted butter (at room temperature)
1 ½ cups granulated sugar
2 ¾ cups all-purpose flour
3 tsp baking powder

1 tsp salt
¾ cup champagne
6 egg whites

Instructions

1. Preheat oven to 350°F.
2. Line the cupcake pan.
3. Beat butter until smooth. Add sugar until very light and fluffy.
4. In a separate bowl, sift flour, baking powder, and salt together.
5. Alternate adding dry ingredients and champagne into the butter mixture.
6. In a separate mixing bowl, beat egg whites until stiff peaks form. (This can take a few minutes, so be patient.)
7. Fold a third of the whites into the batter. Then fold in remaining egg whites. (Do this in two steps to prevent over-mixing and deflating your egg whites.)
8. Fill the papers half way with a spoon or scoop.
9. Bake for 20 minutes for full-size, or 12 minutes for mini cupcakes. Let cool.

*Recommended frosting: Champagne buttercream. Garnish with orange zest.

Banana Split Cupcakes

Ingredients

⅓ cup butter, at room temperature
⅓ cup granulated sugar
1 large egg
¼ tsp vanilla extract
⅓ cup self-rising flour
¼ tsp baking powder

1 mashed banana (Super ripe
   bananas will be sweeter and
   easier to mash.)
7 ½ tsp rum
maraschino cherries

Instructions

1. Preheat oven to 350°F.
2. Line the cupcake pan.
3. Beat the butter until smooth. Add sugar until light and fluffy.
4. Add the egg and beat until fully incorporated.
5. Add the vanilla extract.
6. Fold in the flour and baking powder.
7. Add the banana and fold until evenly distributed.
8. Fill the papers about half way with a spoon or scoop.
9. Bake for 15–20 minutes for full-size, or 12–14 minutes for mini cupcakes.
10. Remove pan and let cupcakes cool.
11. Pour hot rum over the cupcakes. You can create a fill-hole or let it soak into the cake.
12. Let cool and fill center of cupcake with a maraschino cherry. Use half a cherry for mini cupcakes.

*Recommended frosting: Banana Buttercream. Garnish with a banana slice, drizzle with chocolate and add chopped nuts or sprinkles . . . or both!

Chocolate Covered Raspberry Cupcakes

Ingredients

1 ⅓ cups all-purpose flour
¼ tsp baking soda
2 tsp baking powder
¾ cups cocoa powder
⅛ tsp salt
3 tbsp butter at room temperature
1 ½ cups granulated sugar

2 eggs at room temperature.
2 tsp Vanilla-flavored Vodka
1 cup milk

Chocolate covered cherry truffles (optional):
½ cup butter, softened

3–4 cups powder sugar
2 tsp raspberry-flavored Svedka vodka
2 drops red food coloring
Cocoa powder to dust

Instructions

1. Preheat oven to 350°F.
2. Line the cupcake pan.
3. Add dry ingredients to a bowl (flour, baking soda, baking powder, cocoa, salt). Set aside.
4. Beat butter until smooth. Add sugar and mix until light and fluffy.
5. Add eggs, one at a time until blended.
6. Add vodka and milk to mixture.
7. Add dry mixture to wet, about ½ cup at a time. Mix until well combined.
8. Fill papers halfway; drop one truffle into the middle of cupcake batter.
9. Bake for 20–25 minutes for full-size, or 12 minutes for mini cupcakes.
10. Cool completely.
11. If you chose to omit the chocolate truffle center, you can create a fill-hole and instead stuff the cooled cupcake with a maraschino cherry. Add about ½ tsp of maraschino cherry juice to center as well.

*Recommended frosting: Chocolate ganache or Cherry Coke frosting. Top with a maraschino cherry and drizzle with chocolate syrup.

Pina Colada Cupcakes

Ingredients

½ cup butter at room temperature
1 cup granulated sugar
2 eggs at room temperature
Contents of ½ vanilla bean (If you can't get your hands on vanilla bean, a tsp of vanilla extract will work.)

½ tsp coconut extract
1 ½ cups all-purpose flour
1 tsp baking powder
¼ cup coconut milk
¼ cup coconut rum
¼ cup shredded coconut
¼ cup pineapple chunks, diced

Instructions

1. Preheat oven to 350°F
2. Line the cupcake pan.
3. Cream butter until smooth. Add sugar and eggs together until fluffy. Add vanilla and coconut extracts and mix until combined.
4. Combine dry ingredients in a bowl. Add half of the dry ingredients, mixing until just combined. Add the milk, then add remaining dry ingredients.
5. Add coconut rum and fold in shredded coconut.
6. Fill papers half-way with spoon or scoop.
7. Bake for 20–25 minutes for full-size, or 12 minutes for mini cupcakes.
8. Let cool completely.
9. Create a fill-hole, and place several pieces of pineapple chunks into center. You can also add a tsp of pineapple juice for extra flavor.

*Recommended frosting: Coconut Buttercream. Garnish with shredded coconut.

Lemon Drop Cupcakes

Ingredients

Approximately 4 lemons, zested
(about ¼ cup zest)
3 tbsp vodka
1 cup unsalted butter (at room
temperature)
1 cup self-rising flour
1 tsp baking powder

1 cup granulated sugar
4 eggs (at room temperature)

Syrup:
5 tbsp vodka
2 tbsp brown sugar
Lemon zest for garnish

Instructions

1. Soak lemon zest in the vodka for an hour before use.
2. Preheat oven to 350°F.
3. Line the cupcake pan.
4. Beat butter until smooth.
5. Sift in flour, baking powder, and sugar into large mixing bowl.
6. Adding only a cup of dry ingredients at a time, use an electric mixer to whisk the batter until light and fluffy.
7. Add in eggs one at a time until well incorporated.
8. Continue to beat the mixture until smooth and pale on medium low speed approximately 2–3 minutes.
9. Fold in soaked lemon zest until well combined.
10. Fill the papers half way with spoon or scoop.
11. Bake for 22 minutes for full-size, or 12 minutes for mini cupcakes.
12. Create fill-holes once cooled.

To make Vodka Syrup: combine vodka and brown sugar into a saucepan. Simmer the syrup for about 5 minutes on low heat. Pour or coat the warm syrup over the cupcake.Cool cupcakes completely before frosting.

*Recommended frosting: Lemoncello Buttercream. Garnish with lemon zest and some coarse sanding sugar.

Margarita Cupcakes

Ingredients

1 ½ cups all-purpose flour
1 ½ tsp baking powder
¼ tsp salt
½ cup unsalted butter, at room temperature
1 cup granulated sugar

2 eggs, at room temperature
Zest and juice of 1 ½ limes
¼ tsp vanilla extract
5 tbsp tequila, plus extra for brushing
½ cup buttermilk

Instructions

1. Preheat the oven to 325°F.
2. Line the cupcake pan.
3. In a medium bowl, whisk together the flour, baking powder, and salt. Set aside.
4. With an electric mixer, beat the butter until smooth. Add sugar until pale, light, and fluffy.
5. Add eggs, one at a time, making sure they are well incorporated before adding the next.
6. Add the lime zest, lime juice, vanilla extract, and tequila. Mix until combined. (The batter will start to look like it's curdled. Just keep mixing, it will come back together.)
7. Add the dry ingredients a cup at a time, alternating with the buttermilk. Mix only until just incorporated.
8. Fill papers halfway with a spoon or scoop.
9. Bake for 20–25 minutes for full-size, or 12 minutes for mini cupcakes.
10. Allow cupcakes to cool for 5 to 10 minutes, and then remove to a cooling rack. Brush the tops of the cupcakes with the 1 to 2 tbsp of tequila.
11. Set the cupcakes aside to cool completely before frosting them.

*Recommended frosting: Margarita Buttercream. Garnish with lime zest and some coarse sea salt.

French Toast Maple Bacon Cupcakes

Ingredients

½ cup cooked bacon, finely chopped†

1 ¼ cups all-purpose flour

¼ tsp baking soda

1 tsp baking powder

½ tsp cinnamon

½ tsp nutmeg

½ tsp salt

¾ cup granulated sugar

⅓ cup vegetable oil

⅔ cup milk

2 tsp vanilla extract

⅔ cup maple syrup

Instructions

1. Preheat oven to 350°F.
2. Line the cupcake pan.
3. In a large bowl, sift together flour, baking soda, baking powder, cinnamon, nutmeg, salt, and granulated sugar and set aside.
4. In a small bowl whisk together oil, milk, vanilla, and maple syrup.
5. Fold wet mixture into dry. Add bacon until just combined.
6. Fill papers half full with spoon or scoop.
7. Bake 20–25 minutes for full-size, or 12 minutes for mini cupcakes.
8. Cool completely before frosting.

*Recommended frosting: Maple buttercream, or for the sweetest sweet tooth, you can make the same recipe with a cream cheese frosting. Garnish with some bacon, finely chopped.

† I usually go through an entire package of bacon for these cupcakes! Make sure your bacon is crispy. Avoid cooking on high heat to prevent burning and don't undercook because gelatinous bacon doesn't seem to work well with cupcakes.

Irish Car Bomb Cupcakes

Ingredients

1 cup Guinness stout

1 cup unsalted butter, at room temperature

¾ cup cocoa powder

2 cups all-purpose flour

2 cups granulated sugar

1 ½ tsp baking soda

¾ tsp salt

2 eggs

⅔ cup sour cream

Instructions

1. Preheat oven to 350°F.
2. Line the cupcake pan.
3. Bring the Guinness and butter to a simmer in a heavy, medium saucepan over medium heat. Add the cocoa powder and whisk until the mixture is smooth. Let cool slightly.
4. Whisk the flour, sugar, baking soda, and salt in a large bowl until combined.
5. Using an electric mixer, beat the eggs and sour cream on medium speed until combined. Add the Guinness-chocolate mixture to the egg mixture and beat until just combined. Reduce the speed to low, add the flour mixture, and beat briefly.
6. Fold the batter until completely combined.
7. Fill the cupcake papers with spoon or scoop.
8. Bake for about 17 minutes for full-size, or 12 minutes for mini cupcakes. Let cool.
9. Create a fill-hole and fill center of cupcakes with the whiskey ganache (found in the frosting section for Irish Car Bomb). You can use a decorating bag with a piping tip to help with this process since the ganache tends to be messier than most fillings.

*Recommended Frosting: Baileys® Frosting. Garnish with chocolate shavings or your favorite sprinkles.

S'mores Cupcakes

Ingredients

1 ½ cups all-purpose flour
1 ⅓ cups graham crackers, crushed
2 tsp baking powder
1 ½ tsp salt
1 ½ tsp ground cinnamon
1 ¼ cups unsalted butter, room
  temperature

2 cups light brown sugar
¼ cup honey
6 eggs
2 tsp vanilla extract
¼ cup chocolate
  (or marshmallow) vodka

Instructions

1. Preheat oven to 350°F.
2. Line the cupcake pan.
3. Whisk together flour, graham crackers, baking powder, salt, and cinnamon.
4. With an electric mixer on medium-high speed, cream the butter, brown sugar, and honey until light and fluffy.
5. Reduce speed to medium and beat in the eggs and vanilla. Add the flour mixture until just combined.
6. Fill cupcake papers with spoon or scoop.
7. Bake for about 20–25 minutes for full-size, or 12 minutes for mini cupcakes. Let cool.
8. Brush the chocolate vodka onto each cupcake.

*Recommended Frosting: Marshmallow frosting. Toast frosting lightly with a hand held propane torch.

Red and Black Velvet Cupcakes

Ingredients

4 tbsp unsalted butter (at room temperature)
¾ cup granulated sugar
1 egg
2 ½ tbsp unsweetened cocoa powder
3 tbsp red food coloring†
½ tsp vanilla extract
½ cup buttermilk

1 cup + 2 tbsp all-purpose flour
½ tsp salt
½ tsp baking soda
1 ½ tsp distilled white vinegar
1 cup mini chocolate chips (Mini chocolate chips are best for mini cupcakes. You can use normal sized chips for standard sized cupcakes.)

Instructions

1. Preheat oven to 350°F.
2. Line the cupcake pan.
3. On medium speed, beat the butter and sugar until light and fluffy.
4. Turn the mixer to high and add the egg until well incorporated.
5. In a separate bowl, mix together the cocoa powder, vanilla extract, and red food coloring until thick.
6. Add this mixture to the batter on medium speed until fully combined. (Add more red coloring until you are happy with the final result. Keep in mind that the color will appear darker after being baked. Mixing well will ensure that all the coloring has been incorporated.)
7. Reduce the speed to low and alternate adding the buttermilk and flour, adding about half the amount at a time. Mix well.
8. Add the salt, baking soda, and vinegar. Turn to high and beat for another couple of minutes until completely combined and smooth.

9. Add chocolate chips until just combined. (This is what makes these cupcakes red and black velvet. It can be omitted if you prefer, however I highly recommend giving them a shot. It certainly makes for one tasty cupcake!)
10. Fill cupcake papers with spoon or scoop.
11. Bake for about 20–25 minutes for full-size, or 12 minutes for mini cupcakes. Let cool.

*Recommended Frosting: Cream cheese frosting. Garnish with chopped up chocolate chips or leave plain.

†Gel coloring will give you the richest red color, or you can purchase red velvet dye at your local cake supply store.

Salted Caramel Toddy Cupcakes

Ingredients

½ cup + 1 tbsp cocoa powder

½ cup + 1 tbsp hot water

2 ¼ cups all-purpose flour

¾ tsp baking soda

¾ tsp baking powder

½ tsp salt

1 cup + 1 tbsp unsalted butter (at room temperature)

1 ⅔ cups granulated sugar

3 eggs

1 tbsp vanilla extract

¾ cup sour cream

Instructions

1. Preheat oven to 350°F.
2. Line the cupcake pans.
3. Whisk together the cocoa powder and hot water until smooth.
4. In a separate medium bowl, whisk together the flour, baking soda, baking powder, and salt.
5. Combine the butter and sugar in a medium saucepan set over medium heat. Stirring occasionally, cook until the mixture is smooth, and the butter is completely melted. Transfer the mixture to the bowl of an electric mixer and beat on medium-low speed until the mixture is cool, about 4 to 5 minutes.
6. Add the eggs one at a time, mixing well after each addition.
7. Add the vanilla and the cocoa mixture; beat until smooth.
8. Alternate adding the flour and sour cream, adding a little bit each time. Mix until just incorporated.
9. Fill cupcake papers with spoon or scoop.
10. Bake for 20 minutes for full-size, or 12 minutes for mini cupcakes. Let cool.

*Recommended Frosting: Caramel Frosting. Garnish with coarse sea salt and drizzle with caramel.

Cherry Coke Cupcakes

Ingredients

1 ½ cups all-purpose flour
3 tbsp cocoa powder
½ tsp baking soda
¼ tsp salt
¾ cup granulated sugar

½ cup unsalted butter, at room temperature
1 egg
½ cup buttermilk
½ cup water
1 tsp Coke flavoring

(you can find this at your local cake supply store)
1 ½ tsp vanilla extract
Maraschino cherries

Instructions

1. Preheat the oven to 350°F.
2. Line the cupcake pans.
3. Sift together flour, cocoa powder, baking soda, and salt in a small bowl and set aside.
4. In a separate bowl, combine the sugar and butter and beat on medium-high until light and creamy.
5. Add the egg and continue to beat for another minute.
6. In a small bowl, combine the buttermilk, water, coke flavoring, and vanilla extract.
7. Alternate adding the flour mixture and coke flavor mixture into the butter mixture, adding a little bit at a time. Mix until just combined.
8. Fill cupcake papers with spoon or scoop.
9. Bake for 18–20 minutes for full-size, or 12–14 minutes for mini cupcakes.
10. Cut a small hole in the center of the cupcakes and push a maraschino cherry into the center. Use only half a cherry for mini cupcakes.

*Recommended Frosting: Cherry Buttercream. Garnish with a cherry or some sprinkles.

Mojito Cupcakes

Ingredients

½ cup white rum
Fresh mint sprigs
1 ½ cups all-purpose
  flour
1 ½ tsp baking
  powder
¼ tsp salt

½ cup unsalted
  butter, at room
  temperature
1 cup granulated
  sugar
2 eggs, at room
  temperature

Zest and juice of
  1 ½ limes
¼ tsp vanilla extract
1 tsp mint extract
2 tbsp white rum
½ cup buttermilk

Instructions

1. Combine the ½ cup rum and mint sprigs in a small bowl and set aside.
2. Preheat oven to 350°F.
3. Line the cupcake pans.
4. In a medium bowl, whisk together the flour, baking powder, and salt.
5. In a separate bowl, use an electric mixer on medium-high speed and beat the butter and sugar together until pale and fluffy.
6. Add the eggs one at a time, making sure they are well incorporated.
7. Add the lime zest, lime juice, vanilla extract, mint extract, and rum. Mix until combined. (The lime juice may make the mixture look curdled. Just keep mixing it will smooth out again.)
8. Add the dry ingredients a little at a time, alternating with the buttermilk. Mix until just incorporated.
9. Fill cupcake papers with spoon or scoop.
10. Bake for 22–25 minutes for full-size cupcakes, or 12–14 minutes for mini cupcakes.
11. Brush the tops of the cupcakes with the rum/mint mixture.

*Recommended Frosting: Mint Buttercream. Garnish with a mint leaf.

Spiced Pumpkin Cupcakes

Ingredients

4 cups cake flour
1 tsp baking soda
1 tbsp + 1 tsp baking powder
1 tsp salt
2 tsp ground cinnamon
1 tbsp ground ginger
1 tsp freshly grated nutmeg
¼ tsp ground cloves
1 cup (2 sticks) unsalted butter, room temperature
2 ½ cups packed light-brown sugar
4 large eggs
1 cup buttermilk
1 ½ cups canned pumpkin (Be sure to get actual canned pumpkin and not pumpkin pie filling.)

Instructions

1. Preheat oven to 350°F.
2. Line the cupcake pans.
3. Sift together flour, baking soda, baking powder, salt, and spices.
4. In a separate bowl on medium-high speed, cream butter and brown sugar until pale and fluffy. Add eggs, one at a time, beating until just incorporated.
5. Alternate adding the flour mixture and buttermilk, adding a little bit at a time.
6. Add pumpkin; beat until just combined.
7. Fill cupcake papers with spoon or scoop.
8. Bake for 20 minutes for full-sized, or 12 minutes for mini cupcakes. Let cool.

*Recommended Frosting: Cream Cheese Frosting. Garnish with a sprinkling of cinnamon.

Spiked Lemonade Cupcakes

Ingredients

1 ½ cups all-purpose flour
1 tsp baking powder
½ tsp salt
2 ounces (½ stick) unsalted butter, at room temperature
2 ounces cream cheese, at room temperature

1 cup granulated sugar
3 large eggs
2 tbsp Limoncello
½ cup buttermilk
¼ cup lemon juice
Zest of one lemon

Instructions

1. Preheat the oven to 350°F.
2. Line the cupcake pans.
3. In a medium bowl, combine the flour, baking powder, and salt.
4. In a separate bowl, with an electric mixer, beat the butter, cream cheese and sugar on medium speed until light and creamy.
5. Add the eggs, one at a time, beating well after each addition.
6. Add the Limoncello.
7. Alternate adding flour mixture and buttermilk, adding a little bit at a time.
8. Add the lemon juice and zest and mix on low speed just until incorporated.
9. Fill cupcake papers with spoon or scoop.
10. Bake for 25 minutes for full-size, or 12 minutes for mini cupcakes. Let cool.
11. Create a fill-hole in each cupcake and fill with the lemon curd. (Use the lemon curd recipe in the frosting section under Spiked Lemonade.)

*Recommended Frosting: Lemon Buttercream. Garnish with coarse sugar.

Buckeye Cupcakes

Ingredients

½ cup (1 stick) unsalted butter, at room temperature
2 oz. bittersweet chocolate, chopped
½ cup cocoa powder
¾ cup all-purpose flour
½ tsp baking soda
¾ tsp baking powder
2 eggs
¾ cup granulated sugar
1 tsp vanilla extract
½ tsp table salt
½ cup (4 oz.) sour cream

Instructions

1. Preheat oven to 350°F.
2. Line the cupcake pans.
3. Combine butter, chocolate, and cocoa in medium heatproof bowl. Set bowl over saucepan containing barely simmering water. Heat mixture until butter and chocolate are melted and whisk until smooth and combined. (Be patient, this takes some time. Heat too quickly and the mixture will seize, becoming clumpy.)
4. Whisk flour, baking soda, and baking powder in small bowl.
5. Whisk eggs in second medium bowl. Add sugar, vanilla, and salt until fully incorporated. Add cooled chocolate mixture and whisk until combined.
6. Sift flour mixture over chocolate mixture a little bit at a time and whisk until combined. Whisk in sour cream until combined, then sift remaining flour mixture over and whisk until batter is thick.
7. Fill cupcake papers with spoon or scoop.
8. Bake for 18–20 minutes for full-size, or 12–14 minutes for mini cupcakes.

*Recommended Frosting: Chocolate ganache swirl with a peanut butter center.

62

Tiramisu Cupcakes

Ingredients

1 ¼ cups cake flour
¾ tsp baking powder
½ tsp coarse salt
¼ cup milk

1 ½ tsp vanilla
 extract
4 tbsp unsalted
 butter (at room
 temperature)

3 whole eggs + 3 egg
 yolks (at room
 temperature)
1 cup granulated
 sugar

Instructions

1. Preheat oven to 325°F.
2. Line the cupcake pans.
3. Sift together cake flour, baking powder, and salt.
4. Heat milk and vanilla extract in a small saucepan over medium heat just until bubbles appear around the edge. Remove from heat. Whisk in butter until melted. Let stand 15 minutes.
5. With an electric mixer, whisk together whole eggs, yolks, and sugar.
6. Set mixing bowl over a pan of simmering water (double boiler), and whisk by hand until sugar is dissolved and mixture is warm, approximately 6 minutes. Remove bowl from heat.
7. With an electric mixer on high speed, whisk until mixture is fluffy, pale yellow, and holds a stiff peak when the whisk is lifted.
8. Gently fold flour mixture into the egg mixture in three batches; stir ½ cup batter into the strained milk mixture to thicken, and then fold milk mixture into the remaining batter until just combined.
9. Fill the cupcake papers with spoon or scoop.
10. Bake for 18–20 minutes for full-size, or 12–14 minutes for mini cupcakes. Let cool.
11. Create fill-hole and pour the coffee syrup into center. (This recipe is under Tiramisu in Frosting Section)

*Recommended Frosting: Mascarpone Frosting. Garnish with a dusting of cocoa powder

Birthday Cake Cupcakes

Ingredients

2 ¾ cups all-purpose flour
½ cup cake flour
1 tbsp baking powder
1 tsp salt
1 cup unsalted butter, at room temperature
2 ¼ cups granulated sugar
1 ½ tsp vanilla extract
3 eggs
1 egg white
1 cup whole milk
Approximately 4 or 5 tbsp rainbow sprinkle jimmies. (Nonpareils, or the tiny balls, will bleed their colors into the cake, turning it a dirty brown. Be sure to use the jimmies, or the long skinny sprinkles instead.)

Instructions

1. Preheat oven to 350°F.
2. Line the cupcake pans.
3. Whisk together both flours, baking powder, and salt. Set aside.
4. With an electric mixer, beat together the butter, sugar, and vanilla until light and fluffy.
5. Add the eggs and egg white, one at a time, beating until fully incorporated.
6. Alternate adding the flour mixture with the milk, adding a little bit at a time.
7. Fold in the sprinkles by hand.
8. Fill cupcake papers with spoon or scoop.
9. Bake for 20–25 minutes for full-size, or 12–14 minutes for mini cupcakes. Let cool.

*Recommended Frosting: Strawberry Buttercream. Garnish with rainbow sprinkles.

66

'Tucky Derby Pie Cupcakes

Ingredients

1 ½ cups cake flour
½ tsp baking powder
¼ tsp baking soda
½ tsp salt
¾ cup chopped walnuts (Walnuts are customary but you can replace this with any nuts you prefer.)
½ cup semisweet mini chocolate chips

½ cup buttermilk, at room temperature
2 tbsp bourbon
½ cup unsalted butter, at room temperature
¾ cup granulated sugar
¼ cup light brown sugar
2 eggs (at room temperature)

Instructions

1. Preheat oven to 350°F.
2. Line the cupcake pans.
3. In a medium bowl, sift together the flour, baking powder, and baking soda. Whisk in the salt, walnuts, and chocolate chips. Set aside.
4. In a small cup, whisk together the buttermilk and bourbon, and set aside.
5. Using an electric mixer, beat the butter and both sugars on medium speed until light and fluffy.
6. Add the eggs, one at a time, beating each until incorporated.
7. Alternate adding the flour mixture with the milk. Mix until just combined.
8. Fill cupcake papers with spoon or scoop.
9. Bake for 18–20 minutes for full-size, or 12–14 minutes for mini cupcakes.
10. Create a fill-hole and pour in the butter-bourbon glaze. Recipe is under Derby Pie in frostings section.

*Recommended Frosting: Vanilla Buttercream. Garnish with chopped up walnuts, mini chocolate chips, and drizzle with caramel and chocolate syrup.

Alcoholic Frostings, Fillings, and Fruits

The base for all buttercream frostings is butter, and in most cases, shortening. In order to have perfectly smooth, lump-free frosting, your butter and shortening must be at room temperature. Check out Tips and Tricks for bringing to room temperature more quickly, but certainly don't skip this crucial step!

If you want to add more volume, stability and creaminess to your frosting, you can add shortening, even if it doesn't call for it. Be warned that too much shortening and you will be left with a greasy aftertaste.

Each cupcake recipe has a recommended frosting; however, use your own preferences and creativity to play around with variations.

Vanilla Buttercream

This is such a versatile recipe, and is essentially the base for all other buttercream recipes. Add some extract or flavor oils, chop up your favorite nut or fruit. Better yet, feel free to add several tablespoons of your favorite liquor to turn this recipe into its adult version. Play around with it, and make it your own!

Ingredients

½ cup (1 stick) unsalted butter, softened

½ cup shortening (not butter flavored)

4 ½ cups powder sugar (approximately)

1 ½ tsp vanilla extract

Tablespoons of water as needed

In a large bowl, beat butter and shortening until creamy. Beat in the powder sugar and vanilla. Add a tablespoon of water until desired consistency is achieved. See Tips and Tricks for the different consistencies, and how to achieve the right thickness.

If you really wanted, you could omit the butter. Just add an additional cup of shortening. This will make for a stiffer, very sweet frosting. If you still want the butter flavor, but not the actual butter, you can always use butter flavor shortening (which will make your frosting an off-white color) or butter flavoring.

Instructions

For pure wedding-white frosting, omit the butter, and instead use clear butter flavoring, and use clear vanilla extract. You can find these at your local craft store or cake supply store.

CRUSTING BUTTERCREAM

Prepare vanilla buttercream. Instead of water, you will use about ½ or ¾ cup of milk. Be warned that crusting buttercream does crust over pretty quickly, so be sure to add any toppings right after you have piped your cupcakes, otherwise they will just bounce off.

Almond Buttercream: Prepare vanilla buttercream, and use ½ to ¾ tsp almond extract as well. For a more pure almond flavor, you can omit the vanilla.

Chocolate Buttercream: Prepare vanilla buttercream except use 4 cups powder sugar, ½ cup baking cocoa, and 6–7 tbsp milk.

Lemon Buttercream: Prepare vanilla buttercream. Add ½ to ¾ tsp lemon extract. For an extra burst of flavor, add some lemon zest.

Orange Buttercream: Prepare vanilla buttercream. Add ½ to ¾ tsp of orange extract. For an extra burst of flavor, add some orange zest as well.

Peanut Butter Buttercream: Prepare vanilla buttercream. Add ½ cup peanut butter and an additional 1 cup of powder sugar.

Cream Cheese Frosting

Ingredients

½ cup (1 stick) unsalted butter, softened
4 oz. cream cheese, softened
2 cups powdered sugar

1 tsp vanilla
3 tbsp white rum (or any of your favorites!)

Whip butter and cream cheese until smooth. Gradually add powder sugar. Add vanilla. Beat frosting for a good 5 minutes. Not only will this make for a smoother, fluffier consistency, but will also make the frosting whiter. Turn this recipe into its spiked version by adding a few tablespoons of your favorite alcohol. I find it works best with vanilla-flavored or standard-flavored vodkas and rum. However, if you prefer cream cheese for your coffee cupcake, add some Kahlua or Baileys® instead.

Chocolate Ganache

Ingredients

4 oz. semisweet chocolate   ½ cup heavy cream

Finely chop the chocolate and transfer it to a heatproof bowl, set aside. Heat the cream in a small saucepan on low heat, stirring constantly until simmering, and pour it over the chocolate. Using a rubber spatula, stir gently until chocolate has melted completely. Let the ganache cool so that it becomes thick. See our Tips and Tricks for the variations on using ganache.

Coconut Frosting

Ingredients

1 cup (2 sticks) unsalted butter, softened

4 cups powdered sugar

¼ cup coconut rum

1 tbsp vanilla

Whip butter until smooth. Gradually add powder sugar. Add rum and vanilla. Add more sugar a spoonful at a time until you achieve the desired consistency.

Margarita Frosting

Ingredients

1 cup (2 sticks) unsalted butter, softened
4 cups powdered sugar
¼ cup tequila
1 tbsp lime extract
Lime zest
Coarse salt

Whip the butter until smooth. Gradually add the powder sugar. Add the lime extract, zest, and tequila until fluffy. Add more sugar a spoonful at a time until you achieve the desired consistency. Garnish with coarse salt.

Coffee Kahlua Frosting

Ingredients

1 cup (2 sticks) unsalted butter, softened
4 cups powdered sugar
¼ cup sour cream

⅛ cup Kahlua
2 heaping tbsp of instant coffee (regular coffee won't work here!)

Whip the butter until smooth. Gradually add the powder sugar. Add the Kahlua, sour cream, and coffee until fluffy. Add more sugar a spoonful at a time until you achieve the desired consistency.

Mimosa Frosting

Ingredients

1 cup (2 sticks) unsalted butter, softened
4 cups powdered sugar
½ tsp vanilla extract
⅛ cup champagne (at room temperature)
Orange zest
2 tsp champagne flavor (optional)

Whip the butter until smooth. Gradually add the powder sugar. Add the champagne and zest until fluffy. The champagne bubbles will break down your frosting, and making it frothy and quite fluid. Just add more sugar a spoonful at a time until you achieve the desired consistency. It's because of this that I like to add champagne flavoring, which can be found at your local cake supply store. It certainly is optional, but gives it an additional kick that I find to be quite nice when paired with the actual champagne.

Banana Split Frosting

Ingredients

¼ cup butter, softened
4 cups powder sugar
½ cup mashed bananas

½ tsp lemon extract
½ tsp vanilla
⅛ cup white rum

Whip butter until smooth. Gradually add the powder sugar. Add the bananas, lemon, and vanilla extract and the white rum until fluffy. Add more sugar a spoonful at a time until you achieve the desired consistency.

French Toast Maple Bacon Frosting

Ingredients

4 oz. cream cheese, softened

½ cup (1 stick) unsalted butter, softened

4 cups powder sugar

½ tsp salt

½ cup maple syrup

1 tbsp brown sugar

1 tbsp cinnamon

¼ cup bourbon whiskey

8 oz. cooked bacon

Whip cream cheese and butter until smooth. Gradually add powder sugar. Add salt, maple syrup, brown sugar, cinnamon, and bourbon whiskey until fluffy. Add in cooked bacon last. Make sure the bacon has been rendered fairly crispy and that all fat has been drained off. The bacon should be at room temperature and chopped fairly well before adding. Because of the bacon pieces, you will only be able to use round piping tips, perfect for creating dollops. Add more sugar (or liquid) a spoonful at a time until you achieve the desired consistency.

Baileys® Frosting

Ingredients

2 cups (4 sticks) unsalted
   butter, softened

5 cups powdered sugar
6 tbsp Baileys Irish Cream®

Whip butter until smooth. Gradually add powder sugar. Add Baileys®. Add more sugar or liquid one spoonful at a time until you achieve the desired consistency.

Whiskey Ganache Frosting

Ingredients

8 oz. bittersweet chocolate
⅔ cup heavy cream

2 tbsp butter, softened
1 tbsp whiskey

Finely chop the chocolate and transfer it to a heatproof bowl. Set aside. Heat the cream in a small saucepan on low heat, stirring constantly until simmering, and pour it over the chocolate. Using a rubber spatula, stir gently until chocolate has melted completely. Add the butter and whiskey and stir until combined. Let the ganache cool so that it becomes thick. See our Tips and Tricks for the variations on using ganache.

Marshmallow Frosting

Ingredients

8 egg whites
2 cups granulated sugar
½ tsp cream of tartar

⅛ tsp salt
2 tsp vanilla

Set up a double boiler (see Tips and Tricks on how to create this using pots you already own). For this system, use your electric mixer bowl for your top pan. Add egg whites and sugar to the top pan. Over medium heat, by hand, whisk the egg whites and sugar constantly, making sure the sugar is completely dissolved. Add cream of tartar, salt, and vanilla. Continue to whisk until egg whites are warm to the touch. This process ensures that you kill off harmful bacteria. Too warm and you will start to cook your eggs, and not warm enough will mean you will consume raw eggs. Gently lift the whisk and pinch the dripping egg whites to test the temperature. They should feel warm, but not too hot to touch. Transfer the mixture in the mixing bowl to the electric mixer and with the whisk attachment, whisk on high for about 5 minutes or until stiff peaks form. Be patient here and make sure to keep whisking to achieve those stiff peaks. If they are too soft, then when you go to toast your frosting, they will just melt. As indicated in the S'mores cupcake recipe, after piping your cupcakes use a handheld torch to lightly toast the frosting, leaving you with a yummy marshmallow crust.

*This recipe can easily be cut in half, or even quartered for small batches of cupcakes. It may not seem like you're making a lot at first, but once the air gets incorporated, the batch doubles in size. This frosting needs to be used right away. If left out, the outside becomes crusted and grainy and the inside will start to become loose and wet. If you have a lot left over, pipe some dollops of the frosting onto some wax paper on a cookie sheet and cook in the oven at 350°F for a few minutes, creating hard meringue cookies!

Salted Caramel Frosting

Ingredients

1 cup (2 sticks) unsalted butter, softened

8 oz. cream cheese, softened

½ cup caramel sauce

5 cups powdered sugar

¼ cup caramel rum

½ tbsp salt

Whip the butter and cream cheese until smooth. Pour in the caramel sauce and beat until combined. Gradually add the powder sugar until fluffy. Add salt and rum. Add in additional sugar one spoonful at a time to achieve the desired consistency.

Cherry Coke Frosting

Ingredients

1 cup (2 sticks) unsalted butter, softened

4 cups powdered sugar

¼ cup cherry vodka

1 tbsp cherry extract

Whip butter until smooth. Gradually add the powder sugar. Add vodka and cherry extract. You can find this and other unique extract/oils at your local cake supply store. Add additional sugar one spoonful at a time to achieve the desired consistency.

Mojito Frosting

Ingredients

1 ¼ cups (2 ½ sticks) unsalted
   butter, softened
4 ½ cups powder sugar

1 ½ tbsp lime juice
¼ cup white rum

Whip butter until smooth. Gradually add powder sugar until fluffy. Add lime juice and white rum. Add additional sugar one spoonful at a time until you achieve the desired consistency. Optionally, you can add 1 or 2 tsp of mint extract. However, since mint is used in the cupcake recipe, it's not necessary. Unless of course you really love mint!

Spiced Pumpkin Frosting

Ingredients

1 cup (2 sticks)
unsalted butter,
softened

12 oz. cream cheese,
softened

4 cups powder sugar
¾ tsp vanilla extract
1 tsp cinnamon
½ tsp cloves
½ tsp ginger

¼ cup pumpkin
schnapps*, or
cinnamon whiskey

Whip butter and cream cheese until smooth. Gradually add powder sugar until fluffy. Add vanilla, cinnamon, cloves, ginger, and alcohol. Add additional sugar one spoonful at a time to achieve the desired consistency.

*Pumpkin schnapps tends to be seasonal, and does not have a high alcohol content. You can opt for a cinnamon whiskey instead, or stick with just plain vodka or rum.

Spiked Lemonade Curd

Ingredients

Zest of 2 lemons
½ cup lemon juice
¼ cup granulated sugar

1 egg + 1 egg yolk
2 tbsp lemon vodka

In a medium saucepan, mix the lemon zest, juice, and sugar and bring to a simmer over medium heat. In a small bowl, whisk together the egg and egg yolk. Whisk the lemon mixture into the eggs, stirring constantly. Move mixture back into the saucepan and place over medium heat, whisking constantly until it thickens. Remove from the heat, add vodka, stir, and let cool completely.

Limoncello Frosting

Ingredients

¼ cup (½ stick) unsalted butter, softened

4 oz. cream cheese, softened

⅛ cup Limoncello

3 ½ cups powder sugar

Whip butter and cream cheese until smooth. Gradually add powder sugar until fluffy. Add Limoncello. Add additional sugar one spoonful at a time to achieve the desired consistency, or in this case, more Limoncello. For a more rich lemon flavor, add some lemon zest.

Whipped Peanut Butter Frosting

Ingredients

5 tbsp unsalted butter, softened
1 cup creamy peanut butter
3 cups powdered sugar
cup heavy cream

¾ tsp vanilla extract
¼ tsp salt
¼ cup whipped cream vodka

Whip butter and peanut butter until smooth. Alternate adding powder sugar with the heavy cream. Add salt, vodka, and vanilla. Beat well until nice and fluffy. Be patient since this can take 5 minutes or more. Add more sugar or even more peanut butter one spoonful at a time to achieve the desired consistency, making sure to beat well after any incorporation so that frosting becomes light and fluffy.

Coffee-Marsala Syrup

Ingredients

⅓ cup + 1 tbsp freshly brewed
   very strong coffee/espresso

1 oz. marsala wine
¼ cup granulated sugar

Stir together hot coffee, marsala, and sugar until sugar is dissolved. Let cool. Brush this syrup onto the cupcakes after they have cooled.

Mascarpone Frosting

Ingredients

1 cup heavy cream
8 oz. mascarpone cheese, softened

1 cup powder sugar
¼ cup Baileys®

Whip heavy cream until stiff peaks form (be careful not to overbeat, or cream will be grainy). In another bowl, whisk together mascarpone and powder sugar until smooth. Gently fold whipped cream and Baileys® into mascarpone mixture until completely incorporated. Use right away!

Birthday Cake Frosting

Ingredients

1 cup (2 sticks) unsalted butter, softened

1 cup shortening

4 cups powder sugar

1 cup fresh strawberries, rinsed, hulled, and coarsely chopped

1 tsp strawberry flavoring

¼ cup strawberry vodka

Whip butter and shortening until smooth. Gradually add powder sugar until fluffy. Add strawberries, vodka, and flavoring. Add additional sugar one spoonful at a time to achieve the desired consistency. Keep in mind that the strawberry chunks mean you will only be able to use a round piping tip when it's time to decorate your cupcakes!

Vanilla-Bourbon Frosting

Ingredients

1 cup (2 sticks) unsalted butter, softened

2 ½ cups powder sugar

Pinch of salt

1 tbsp vanilla extract

⅛ cup bourbon

Whip butter until smooth. Gradually add powder sugar. Add the vanilla and bourbon, mixing until incorporated. Add additional sugar one spoonful at a time to achieve the desired consistency.

Butter-Bourbon Glaze

Ingredients

2 tbsp unsalted butter
¼ cup granulated sugar

1 tbsp + 1 tsp bourbon

Place the butter, sugar, and bourbon in a small bowl and microwave for 1 minute, or until the sugar is dissolved. Stir and let sit for about 15 to 20 minutes so that the glaze thickens slightly.

Spiked Jams

Ingredients

8 cups cherries, pitted and
   stemmed
½ cup water
1 tbsp Fruit-Fresh
1 tbsp vanilla

1 tsp almond extract
1 ¾ oz. package "no sugar
   needed" pectin
½ cup amaretto

CHERRY AMARETTO JAM

If you really want to create some cocktail-twisting cupcakes, learning to create spiked jams is worth it. Though more time consuming, jams really maintain the integrity of the alcohol and will give your cupcakes a nice little added punch. This is a basic recipe that can be modified and played with to match any of the recipes in this book. Not to mention that even as is, these jams can be used as spreads on toast and scones, and essentially used in any manner that a normal jam would be used.

Instructions

Put cherries, water, Fruit-Fresh, vanilla, and almond extract in a saucepan and bring to a boil. Add the pectin just as it is starting to boil. Stir mixture down and simmer for 5 minutes or so. Break down the cherries with a fork or masher if they don't break down themselves. Add amaretto. Mixture should thicken, though not as much as traditional jams.

*If you choose to can your jam: Wash the jars and put them in a single layer in a big pot and boil them for 10 minutes. Turn off the heat and remove them to dry on a clean towel. Drop the flat lids into the hot (not boiling) water. As you fill each clean, warm, dry jar, wipe the rim, cover with the flat disc, and screw a ring on (not too tight). When they are all jarred, put them back into the pot to boil for 10 more minutes, then put back onto the towel to cool.

Martini Gels

The best part about martini gels is that you can really play around with the intensity of each recipe. For more mild shots, take away some liquor and add more juice. For stiff shots, add more alcohol and take away some juice. Just be warned that these recipes are already pretty stiff, so I suggest you try them out before adding your own spin. Too much alcohol and it will taste like you're taking it straight out of the bottle.

You can also play around with different types of pans and molds. Make sure to always use a non-reactive dish. (Find out more about this under Tips and Tricks.) You can use different types of ice cube trays, cupcake pans, and as you become more skilled, you can try out varieties of chocolate molds. The more edges and detail in the mold, the harder it will be to remove your gelatin, so make sure to grease your pans well, be patient, and in the event you are still struggling, it's safe to soak the bottom of the pan in some hot water to loosen up your gelatin. Just be careful not to let it sit too long, and be prepared for a more slippery jelly shot. If they are too wet, you can always put back in fridge to let set again, outside of the pan.

When you are ready to cut your gels, use an oiled knife. You can also use shaped cutters. Use a spatula to get under the gelatin. Don't get discouraged if it breaks and isn't perfect. Cutting gelatin perfectly takes practice, and the final product will taste good no matter what!

Berry Citrus Martini Gel

Ingredients

First layer:
1 packet Knox unflavored gelatin
1 packet (3 oz.) berry-flavored
   gelatin

1 cup hot (boiling is okay) water
6 oz. blackberry vodka

In a small mixing bowl, sprinkle the Knox and the flavored gelatin into very hot water and stir until completely dissolved. This is a very important step! If you don't let the gelatins dissolve, you will end up with a tough, gummy layer in your final product. Let cool for about 5 minutes and then mix in the vodka. Grease a non-reactive dish with oil (vegetable works best), and wipe out with a paper towel. Pour berry mixture in and chill in refrigerator for at least 2 hours.

Ingredients

Second layer:
4 packets Knox unflavored gelatin
1 cup hot (boiling is okay) water
½ cup sugar

1 cup lemon vodka (or rum, or
   gin; you can substitute with any
   lemon-flavored favorite!)
⅔ cup lemon juice

Bloom the gelatin in the hot water by sprinkling it on top. Give it a gentle mix and let sit. After a few minutes, stir until completely dissolved. Add the sugar and stir until fully dissolved. Add the vodka and lemon juice, stirring well. Let mixture sit to cool. Too hot and it will dig a hole in your first layer when you pour it in.Very carefully and slowly, pour the mixture onto your first layer (making sure your first layer is completely set). Chill in refrigerator for at least 2 hours.

Summer Breeze Martini Gel

Ingredients

⅔ cup Rose's lime syrup (This is a mixing syrup that you will find at your liquor store.)

Do not substitute this with lime juice!)

2 tbsp sugar
½ cup water

2 packets Knox gelatin
¾ cup tequila
½ cup Blue Curaçao

Pour lime syrup, sugar, and water in a saucepan. Bloom the gelatin by sprinkling over the top the mixture. Allow gelatin to soak for a few minutes. Over very low heat, stir constantly until completely dissolved. Remove from heat and stir in tequila and Blue Curaçao. Pour into a non-reactive, greased pan and let chill in refrigerator for at least 2 hours. When ready to cut, use a greased knife.

Cosmo Girl Martini Gel

Ingredients

¾ cup cranberry juice
¼ cup Rose's lime juice
3 packets unflavored Knox gelatin
1¼ cup orange flavored vodka
⅓ cup Grand Marnier (This is for a classic Cosmopolitan. Substitute if you must)
Lime zest for garnish, if desired

Pour the cranberry and lime juices in a small saucepan. Bloom gelatin by sprinkling it over the juices. Let soak for a few minutes. Over very low heat, stir constantly until completely dissolved. Stir in the liquors. Pour into greased, non-reactive pan and let set in refrigerator for at least 2 hours. When ready to cut, use a greased knife.

Spiked Lemonade Martini Gel

Ingredients

First layer:
½ cup water
1 packet Knox gelatin

½ cup berry flavored gin (Use your favorite fruit for this one!)

In a small saucepan, add water. Bloom gelatin by sprinkling it on top of the water. Allow to sit for a few minutes. Over low heat, stir constantly until gelatin is completely dissolved. Remove from heat, and stir in gin. Pour into a non-reactive greased pan. Let set in refrigerator for at least 2 hours.

Ingredients

Second layer:
⅔ cup water
⅔ cup lemonade

2 packets Knox gelatin
⅔ cup vodka

In a small saucepan, add water and lemonade. Bloom gelatin by sprinkling it over the mixture. Allow gelatin to soak for a few minutes. Over low heat, stir constantly until gelatin is completely dissolved. Remove from heat and stir in vodka. After first layer has completely set, slowly and carefully pour the mixture over the first layer. Make sure to let mixture cool before pouring over first layer. Let set in refrigerator for at least 2 hours. When ready to cut, use a greased knife.

Other Confections

The world of alcoholic confections is endless, and the options and variations of each recipe would require a whole new book! Here are a few of my other favorite ways to add alcohol to confections. You can play around with these recipes by adding extracts, changing around the flavors, and getting creative with dips, frostings, syrups, etc. I include some ideas on how to change up each recipe to help get you started!

Marshmallows

Ingredients

3 packets Knox unflavored gelatin
½ cup cold water
2 cups granulated sugar
⅔ cup light Karo® syrup

¼ cup water
¼ tsp salt
¾ cup Baileys®
1 tbsp vanilla extract
1 bag powder sugar

Instructions

1. Bloom gelatin by sprinkling it over ½ cup cold water in a large bowl. Soak for 5 minutes.
2. Combine sugar, syrup, and ¼ cup water in a saucepan. Bring to a rapid boil and boil hard for a good minute.
3. Pour sugar mixture over gelatin. Add salt and beat on high for 12 minutes. Mixture will become very thick, and look like white, melted marshmallows.
4. Add Baileys® and vanilla. Mix until combined.
5. Line a 9x9-inch pan with plastic wrap. Pour in a little vegetable oil and wipe down with a napkin. Be liberal and make sure to get all the nooks and crannies. It will make removal much easier and cleaner. Pour gelatin mixture into pan and refrigerate for at least 2 hours.
6. With powder sugar in a bowl, liberally dust a flat surface. Remove marshmallows from fridge and turn them out onto dusted surface and remove plastic. Place a handful of powder sugar on top of the marshmallows and brush it around the top and sides to eliminate sticky spots. Using a well-oiled knife, cut marshmallows into 1-inch cubes (or larger if you prefer). Throw the pieces into bowl of powder sugar and mix well, making sure all sides are coated to prevent sticking.
7. Store marshmallows at room temperature in an air tight container.

BAILEYS® MARSHMALLOWS

Variations: Dip your marshmallows in a chocolate ganache. Make cotton candy (or any flavored) marshmallows using extracts and oils. Play around with other liquors like Kahlua or rum. Alcoholic marshmallows make phenomenal s'mores, and are great fun for creating adult hot chocolate!

Pudding Shots

Ingredients

1 box of instant chocolate
   pudding
¾ cup milk
edible chocolate shells

¼ cup vodka
½ cup Kahlua
8 oz. extra creamy Cool Whip

Prepare the pudding by whisking it into the milk. Make sure it is completely dissolved. Add alcohols. Fold in Cool Whip until well combined. Pour your pudding mixture into edible chocolate shells (available at most grocery stores or cake supply stores) or in little plastic cups (that you can purchase at your local liquor store). Let set in freezer overnight.

MOCHA PUDDING SHOTS

Variations: With all the different flavor varieties available in instant pudding, it really is that simple! Make cookies and cream pudding shots by using the cookies pudding mix, and substituting the vodka and Kahlua for chocolate liqueur or chocolate rum. Fancy up a pistachio recipe by adding chopped up pistachios to your pudding mix. Serve in martini, wine, or champagne glasses for a classier touch.

Spiked Slushy

Ingredients

1 ½ cups diced, frozen peaches
1 ½ cups diced, frozen pineapple
½ cup coconut rum
½ cup orange vodka
½ cup peach schnapps
1 or 2 cups of ice cubes
Splash of grenadine
Maraschino cherries for garnish

Instructions

1. In a blender or food processor, add the fruit, liquors, and blend on high speed until smooth, about 1 minute.
2. Add ice cubes until desired consistency.
3. Divide mixture into glasses and add a splash of grenadine. Garnish with a cherry.

CARIBBEAN FROZEN COCKTAIL

Variations: Pour your mixture into popsicle molds and freeze overnight! (Keep in mind you may want to add more juice and a little less alcohol in order for it to freeze.) Put mixture into an ice cream chiller and create a more realistic slushy texture. Switch up the fruit and have a berry blend instead! If you try to freeze your mixture and it doesn't work, then add more juice and try freezing again!

Index

About the Author

I was born and raised in Cleveland, Ohio. Growing up, I was always encouraged to explore in the kitchen, and often could be found with my head in a Betty Crocker book, whipping up desserts.

I went to college for communications, but after completing internships and entry-level work, I realized that my true passion was as an entrepreneur. I dabbled in a lot of interests and really struggled to find my "calling."

During my yearlong backpacking tour overseas, I came up with the idea of alcoholic cupcakes after eating a Daiquiri cupcake and commenting out loud . . . "I'm going to get drunk off a cupcake!" The worker behind the counter simply replied "Oh no, all the alcohol bakes out . . ." and just as quickly I thought, *Well, how cool would it be if you really could get drunk off a cupcake?*

When I came back home to the States, I immediately started tinkering with recipes and ideas. Once I had a few good ones under my belt, I started to make sales, and just like that, it took off! That was in August of 2011.

We immediately applied for proprietary protection, and are so proud to say we are patent pending! We also have been the pioneers of new liquor laws that regulate the use of alcohol in confections. Being one of the first companies to apply for this type of license means we are paving the way for other companies to use alcohol in untraditional forms.

We are sold in bars and restaurants all over the greater Cleveland area, and can also be found in major sporting and concert venues.

In 2014 we opened our first shop in Cleveland, and have been working with other entrepreneurs in other states so that we can start expansion and possible franchise options.

I currently live in Cleveland, Ohio, with my husband and two children.